Bill Clinton

by Grace Hansen

ABDO
UNITED STATES
PRESIDENT BIOGRAPHIES
Kids

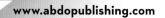
www.abdopublishing.com

Published by Abdo Kids, a division of ABDO, PO Box 398166, Minneapolis, Minnesota 55439.

Copyright © 2015 by Abdo Consulting Group, Inc. International copyrights reserved in all countries. No part of this book may be reproduced in any form without written permission from the publisher.

Printed in the United States of America, North Mankato, Minnesota.

052014

092014

THIS BOOK CONTAINS
RECYCLED MATERIALS

Photo Credits: AP Images, Clinton Family Historical Collection, Corbis, Thinkstock, Shutterstock, © Wasted Time R at en.wikipedia p.7, © Jstone p.11, © spirit of america p.13,15,17,21 / Shutterstock
Cover photo courtesy of William J. Clinton Presidential Library

Production Contributors: Teddy Borth, Jennie Forsberg, Grace Hansen

Design Contributors: Candice Keimig, Laura Rask, Dorothy Toth

Library of Congress Control Number: 2013953025

Cataloging-in-Publication Data

Hansen, Grace.

 Bill Clinton / Grace Hansen.

   p. cm. -- (United States president biographies)

ISBN 978-1-62970-087-8 (lib. bdg.)

Includes bibliographical references and index.

1. Clinton, Bill, 1946- --Juvenile literature. 2. Presidents--United States--Biography--Juvenile literature. I. Title.

973.929--dc23

[B]   2013953025

Table of Contents

Early Life 4

Family 10

Becoming President 12

Presidency 16

More Facts 22

Glossary 23

Index 24

Abdo Kids Code. 24

Early Life

Bill Clinton was born on August 19, 1946. He was born in Hope, Arkansas.

Arkansas

5

Clinton was a good
student. He was also
a good saxophone player.

Clinton went to college

and law school.

9

Family

Clinton has a wife named Hillary. They have a daughter named Chelsea.

CLINTON GLOBAL INITIATIVE

11

Becoming President

Clinton became the **governor** of Arkansas. He was governor for 12 years.

Clinton became the 42nd

US president in 1992.

15

Presidency

Clinton was president
for eight years. The US
did well in those years.

The **economy** was good.

The US also enjoyed

peaceful years.

19

Clinton was a strong leader.

He was a popular president.

21

More Facts

- Clinton had the chance to visit the White House while in high school. There he met President John F. Kennedy. After meeting Kennedy, Clinton knew he wanted to work in politics.

- Clinton's father died in a car accident three months before he was born. When he was 7 years old, his mother married a man named Roger Clinton.

- Clinton memorized Dr. Martin Luther King, Jr.'s speech, "I Have a Dream" when he was a teenager.

Glossary

economy – wealth and resources of a country. If wealth and resources are high, the economy is doing well.

governor – head of a state in the United States.

popular – well-liked by people in general.

saxophone – a musical instrument. It is usually a brass tube with keys and a mouthpiece.

Index

Arkansas 4, 12

birth 4

college 8

daughter 10

economy 18

governor 12

law school 8

peace 18

president 14, 16, 20

saxophone 6

student 6, 8

wife 10

abdokids.com

Use this code to log on to abdokids.com and access crafts, games, videos and more!

Abdo Kids Code:
UBK0878